Time Management Tool for Executives

By Ade Asefeso MCIPS MBA

Second Edition

ISBN-13: 978-1499589375

ISBN-10: 1499589379

Publisher: AA Global Sourcing Ltd
Website: http://www.aaglobalsourcing.com

Table of Contents

Disclaimer..5

Dedication..6

Chapter 1: Introduction 7

Chapter 2: 5 Reasons Why you Should Learn and Practice Proper Time Management........................11

Chapter 3: 8 Simple Steps to Improve Your Time Management..15

Chapter 4: Helpful Time Management Tools........19

Chapter 5: How and Why you Should Play Time Management Games...23

Chapter 6: How to Teach Your Children about Time Management 27

Chapter 7: Important Information on Time Management..31

Chapter 8: Personal Time Management Tips 35

Chapter 9: Successful Time Management Techniques 39

Chapter 10: The Danger of Not Managing Your Time at the Office..43

Chapter 11: The Importance of Personal Time Management..47

Chapter 12: Time Management Tips to Help you See Success...51

Chapter 13: Time Management Training: What It Entails 55

Chapter 14: The Pros and Cons of Time Management Training in the Workplace..............59

Chapter 15: What to Do With Employees Who Do Not Properly Manage Their Time...........................63

Chapter 16: 101 Ways to Get More Done With Less Stress.................67

Chapter 17: Reducing Stress Through Time Management...............................99

Chapter 18: "Who's the Boss?" 10 Ways to Start Taking Control (Time Management, Goal Setting, Record Tracking).....................103

Chapter 19: What Can Time Management Bring to Your Personal Growth...........................107

Chapter 20: Benefits of Time Management.........111

Chapter 21: Time Management Strategies...........113

Chapter 22: Other Time Management Tools......117

Chapter 23: How to Teaching Time Management to Students..............................121

Chapter 24: Conclusion........................125

Disclaimer

Dedication

This book is dedicated to the hundreds of thousands of incredible souls in the world who have weathered through the up and down of recent recession.

To my family and friends who seems to have been sent here to teach me something about who I am supposed to be. They have nurtured me, challenged me, and even opposed me.... But at every juncture has taught me!

This book is dedicated to my lovely boys, Thomas, Michael and Karl. Teaching them to manage their finance will give them the lives they deserve. They have taught me more about life, presence, and energy management than anything I have done in my life.

Chapter 1: Introduction

Time management is a common problem faced by most of us. Oftentimes, when you are swarmed with multiple tasks at once, it becomes extremely difficult to identify which ones you must complete first. Too often, people eat up what is supposed to be their free time to be able to accomplish all pending tasks in time.

It takes a considerate amount of skill in order to manage your time properly. If you are one of these people, you are usually able to control your time efficiently that you can even finish tasks ahead of time.

Let's try to analyze the importance of Time management in different fields.

Time Management in School

Due to more freedom merited to University students, it can become quite challenging for new students to cope with time management. The liberty to choose your own schedule readily creates a false notion that they can do whatever they want. On the other hand, it reflects one's priorities and how you are able to properly appropriate them into your schedule.

With lack of proper time management, a student will have trouble coping up with deadlines set by professors. Most students would tend to slack off during vacant hours that they end up accomplishing nothing.

If a student has prepared his or her own list of work for the day, he or she will be able to properly allocate the time spent for extracurricular activities and assignments.

Time Management at work

When it comes to your job, proper usage of your time is more particular. This is because you are paid for the hours of service you render to the firm. Hence, companies will try to ensure that each hour you spend at the office is utilized effectively for work. Despite of this, employees still seek out ways to have a break.

If time is not properly managed, employees could easily eat up more time for their "breaks" than what is actually spent on actual work. Hence, the company ends up requiring the employee to do overtime work just to finish a project. If the overtime rendered is reflected on your pay cheque, then good for you. But if not, then you reap the unpleasant effects of poor time management.

The Essence of Time Management

With the varying scenarios presented, it all comes down to one thing, proper time management. It allows you to achieve more in less time as compared to doing things without following a suitable system.

By properly allocating your time, you will be able to finish your tasks much faster. Also, you are able to avoid overlapping tasks that tend to slow you down.

How is efficiency linked to proper time management?

Listing your intended work for the day is more than just there for reminder. Instead, they also remind you in terms of importance and urgency. When you make a list, it is important that you also create a time table for each corresponding task. This way, you are compelled to follow them in the time frame that was indicated to increase efficiency.

Aside from becoming more efficient, you also become more responsible when you learn how to properly manage your time. You can not only set your priorities, but also provide equal time for both work and leisure. Being responsible with your time will work effectively whether in school or work.

Probably the biggest benefit you can get from proper time management is that it improves the quality of your work. When you have ample time to work on a certain task, you will have enough time to determine any mistake and have enough time to correct or improve on it. When you are cramming, you do not have this luxury of revision and hence mostly settle for what you can accomplish under the allowed time frame.

To those who fail to manage their time well, most of them work under pressure or hours before the deadline. Hence, they do not get the chance to check the quality of their work.

These are just a few of the practical reasons why Time Management must be practiced by anyone who wants to become more effective in their field.

Chapter 2: 5 Reasons Why you Should Learn and Practice Proper Time Management

Do you have a problem with time management? If you do, you have two main options. One of those options and often the most popular is to continue on with your normal activities. Unfortunately, doing so may have a negative impact on your personal life, as well as your work life. The other option is to make a change. The good news is that there are number of steps that you can take to improve your time management.

As for what you can do to improve your time management, you will see that a number of different approaches can be taken. Goal setting, to do lists, limiting tasking, prioritizing, and outsourcing are all effective ways to manage your time, but they are also just a few of your options. As for why you should learn and practice proper time management, there are a number of reasons why, five of which are outlined below.

1: It is Easy to Do

As previously summarized, you have a number of different options when looking to make better use of your time. These options are all easy and cost effective ways. In fact, creating goals and task lists for yourself is free of charge. Since it is easy for you to learn and practice proper time management techniques, why would you want to do anything else?

2: It is Important to your Personal Life

As previously stated, having a poor sense of time management has a number of serious consequences, one of those being your personal life. If you regularly pay your bills late, don't make contact with friends, or arrive home later than normal, you may be hurting your personal relationships and often in more ways than you could have ever imagined. Friends, spouses, and romantic partners will likely not want to put up with this behaviour for long.

3: It is Important for Your Job

Poor time management will not only negatively affect your personal life, but your work life as well. If you do not know how to properly manage your time, you may get easily distracted. This may result in you wasting company time. If you are caught doing so repeatedly, you may find yourself terminated from your current position. This can also have a negative impact on your personal life, as it may leave your finances in serious trouble.

4: It is Something That you Can Only Benefit from

Taking the time to learn and practice successful time management techniques can only benefit you, your work, and your personal relationships. Since no money technically needs to be spent on time management tools or training, you have nothing to lose, but everything to gain. It is also important to ask yourself again the important question of "why not?" Why not improve your life with the learning and practicing of time management techniques?

5: The Options that you Have

Once again, it is important to focus on the options that you have when looking to learn and practice proper time management. Creating a set of goals and a task list is easy and free to do. Alarm clocks and timers can also be used to help you make better use of your time. You likely already own a traditional alarm, but your cell phone, computer, and television may also come equipped with alarm clocks as well.

As a reminder, there are a number of other time management tools and techniques that you can easily learn and practice all from the comfort of your own home.

Chapter 3: 8 Simple Steps to Improve Your Time Management

Are you an individual who can't seem to properly manage your time? If you are having problems at home or at work, there is a good chance that your problems may be caused by your inability to properly manage your time.

The good news, however, is that there are a number of steps that you can take to improve your time management. In fact, 8 simple steps that you can take are highlighted below.

1: Know that you Have a Problem

Knowing that you have a time management problem is the first step in changing your behaviour. Although it is typical to be late for work or a social event on occasion, it is something that should not be happening on a daily or a weekly basis. If it is, it is time for you to realize that you may have a problem.

2: Decide to Change

Knowing that you have a time management problem is important, but wanting to change is even more important. You need to set goals for yourself, as these goals can help to provide you with a source of motivation. Sample goals include showing up to work on time for a whole month, being on time for all dinner dates, and so forth.

3: Stick to Your Goals

Creating a number of time management goals for you to meet is advised, but it is important that you don't give up right away or when you are faced with complications. Setting goals simply just isn't enough; you need to stick with them.

4: Create Daily Task Lists

Creating a to-do-list for yourself is an easy way to properly manage your time. In fact, it is one of the easiest approaches that you can take. Outline what you need to do throughout the day. Be sure to list your tasks in order of importance.

5: Rely On Time Management Tools

Properly managing your time is important, but it can be hard for many individuals to get use to, especially right away. If you are one of those individuals, you will want to consider using time management tools to your advantage. In fact, did you know that many cell phones and computers come with alarm clocks, alerts, and so much more?

6: Learn How to Say No

In all honesty, there are times where you may not be able to refuse a project at work or a task at home, but try to not take on more than you can accomplish. If you must, look into using outside help. In the home, this outside help can come from a housecleaner. At the workplace, this outside help can come from a co-worker.

7: Get Organized

Organization is key to being able to properly manage your time. If you are unorganized, you are likely to waste a large amount of time. For example, in the workplace you can waste time by searching for lost or misplaced documents. The same can be said for the home; if you are unorganized, you can spend hours searching for your glasses or car keys.

8: Consider Hiring Professional Help

As previously stated, if you are overwhelmed at home, you may want to call on a professional housecleaner. In addition to taking this approach, there are other professionals that you can target. There are individuals and companies who specialize in teaching others how to effectively manage their time and stay organized.

Chapter 4: Helpful Time Management Tools

Would you like to improve your time management? If you find yourself easily distracted, missing important deadlines, or showing up to important events late, improving your time management may be a good idea. Unfortunately, many individuals do not realize just how much trouble poor time management can cause them.

When it comes to improving time management, many individuals are surprised with all of the options that they have. One of those options is using time management tools to your advantage. If this sounds like an approach that you would like to take, please continue reading on. A number of helpful and successful time management tools that you can benefit from using are outlined below and later in this book for your convenience.

An alarm clock is a simple, yet effective time management tool that you can and should use. What is nice about alarm clocks is that most of us already have them in our homes. Be sure to set your alarm clock to get up in the morning. Consider resetting it five minutes before you must walk out to door to work, set it for when you want to start preparing dinner, and so forth. Although we often associate alarm clocks with getting up in the morning, they can actually be used for so much more.

A task list, also commonly referred to as a to-do-list, is another time management tool that you can and should use to your advantage. What is nice about task lists is that they are free and easy to do. All you need is a piece of a paper and pencil. Outlining everything that you must do for the day is a great way to make sure that you stay focused and on task, which is an important component of managing your time. If you must, keep separate lists for home and work.

Daily, weekly, and monthly planners are other time management tools that can be used. The type of planner that you will use will all depend on your own personal preferences. With that said, many individuals prefer daily planners better, as they often leave more space to create a to-do-list or at least a spot to write down important dates and times. If you do use a daily, weekly, or monthly planner, be sure to keep it with you at all times.

Calendar alert programs are other time management tools that come highly rated and recommended. Calendar alert programs are so much more than just a traditional wall calendar. For the most part, these time management alert tools are found on computers and mobile/cell phones. What you will need to do is enter in an important date and time. When that date and time arrives, you should receive a message on your computer screen or mobile phone screen. Text message and emails may also be sent. These types of programs are often used to remember birthdays, but they can be used on a wide range of other events, projects, and activities.

Finally, another tool that you will want to consider using is that of a time management training seminar. In addition to attending a physical class, you may be able to purchase a seminar in video format. Although some individuals do not consider receiving training a tool, it is an important tool.

There are professionals out there who can share time management tips with you, as well as help you improve your organizational skills.

Chapter 5: How and Why you Should Play Time Management Games

Have you heard of time management games before? If you are an avid internet user, you may have. Unfortunately, many individuals make the mistake of assuming that time management games are just for fun. Some actually go as far to say that time management games are a waste of time.

Yes, they can be in some instances, but did you also know that time management games may be able help you practice managing your time?

Before focusing on the benefits of time management games, namely why you should play them, it is first important to understand what they are. If you perform a standard internet search with the phrase "time management games," you will likely get a number of different results. This is because time management games are used to describe a wide range of different games. They often have different themes, including fishing, basketball, shopping, and so much more. The only difference between traditional computer games and time management games is that you are limited on the amount of time that you have to complete the game.

As for how you can find time management games, you will find that you have a number of different options. As previously stated, you can perform a standard internet search. When doing so, you will likely find websites that allow you to play games online, often free of charge. There are also software programs that you can purchase for time management games.

These programs are available for download online or else you can purchase a software program to install on your computer from a local or online retailer.

As for why you should play time management games, there are number of different reasons. One of those reasons being that they are easy to find. As previously stated, a large number of free time management games can be found online with a standard internet search. Should you wish to purchase your own software, you can, but it is not required. The ability to easily find and play time management games gives you little reason not to.

Also, as previously stated, time management games come in a number of different formats. You can play sports games, traditional arcade games and so much more. No matter what type of games you like to play or what your favourite hobbies are, you should have a number of different games to choose from, especially when you use the internet. In fact, did you know that there are even time management games out there for children?

Perhaps, the greatest reason why you should play time management games is because they can help you learn to make better use of your time. Unfortunately, this is an important point that many individuals do not necessarily think of. For example, some games have you eliminate screens of blocks by clicking on groups of blocks that are the same colour. Many associated these types of games with fun activities, but they can also teach you to think quick on your feet. This can later benefit you in the workplace, as well as at home.

Another reason why time management games should be played is because they are fun. Since you do have a number of different time management games to choose from, you can find the game or games that best fit you and your personality. Although you will be working to make better use of your time, you will also be having fun. Learning how to manage your time is important, but it shouldn't seem like work.

As you can see, playing time management games are more than just about having fun or even wasting time. They are a fun tool that can be used to help you better manage your time. To see if time management games are right for you or if they can really help you better manage your time, see what free games are available for playing online today.

Chapter 6: How to Teach Your Children about Time Management

Are you a parent who is interested in teaching your children the importance of time management? If you are, good for you. Time management is a skill that all children should learn, as it may have a significant impact on their future. Unfortunately, many parents do not take the time to teach their children the importance of proper time use. In fact, some parents don't even realize the importance of time management themselves.

Despite the fact that you are certain that you want to teach your child the importance of time management and ways that they can manage their time, you may be unsure as to how you can go about doing so. The approach that you decide to take should depend on your child's age. Please continue reading on for a few helpful tips.

For toddlers and preschoolers, you can use a timer, like a kitchen timer. This is a fun approach to take, as you are essentially creating your own time management game. What you can do is time your child while they complete an easy task. These tasks can be anything from cleaning their room, getting ready for bed, getting washed up for dinner, and so forth. Just make sure that you set a timer with enough time for your child to reasonably do what you are asking of them.

With toddlers and preschoolers, it is important to remember that your child is still young. It isn't always a good idea to discipline them for taking longer than you expected them to take. Just be sure that you talk to your child about picking up their speed and give them easy to understand tips on how they can go about doing so. At this age, be sure to reward your child for beating the time. This reward can be a simple praise, a hug, or a sticker.

As for elementary school aged children, a timer can still be used, but some children do tend to outgrow this approach. Just be sure to talk to your children about time management, its importance, and the consequences for regularly being late. At around the age of eight or so, children are better able to understand what happens when they don't make proper use of their time.

For teenagers, it is important to talk to your child. You will also want to set a good example. Depending on the circumstances at hand, it may also be a good idea to discipline your child. This is actually important to do with schooling. For example, if your teenager isn't able to get their homework done or if they don't study for a test, they may end up with bad grades.

After a few warnings, consider limiting the amount of time that your teenager is able to spend with their friends or the amount of television they are able to watch. Doing this, even just temporarily, is likely to teach your teenager an important lesson about time management and the elimination of distractions.

In keeping with teaching a teenager the importance of time management, it is important to not just take away privileges, but to also provide education.

Make sure that your teenager understands the importance of time management. In University, your child will be responsible for studying, doing their homework, and other important tasks and they will not have you there to help guide them. The same will be true for the workplace. Unfortunately, this is where many young adults run into problems. Don't let your son or daughter fall victim to poor time management.

As you can see, there are a number of easy ways that you can go about teaching your child the importance of time management, as well as tips that you can share with them. Regardless of your children's ages, the lesson of managing time is one that should be taught. In fact, the sooner that you start teaching your children how to properly manage their time, the better the results will likely be in the long run.

Chapter 7: Important Information on Time Management

Are you an individual who finds it difficult to properly manage your time? If you are, you may be looking to make changes. After all, not having a good sense of time management may have a negative impact on your personal life, as well as your work life. If you are looking to improve your sense of time management, there are a number of steps that you will need to take. These steps should have you making better use of your time in no time at all. A few of these steps are highlighted below for your convenience.

First, be sure to set goals for yourself. In fact, setting goals is the most important thing that you can do. Set a number of goals for yourself, such as getting your home office or work desk organized in two to three days. Another goal that you can set is the goal of arriving to work early, and so forth.

Another important component of improving your sense of time management is knowing that there is only a certain amount of time in the day. This is important to remember when setting goals for yourself. You do not want to overextend yourself either at home or at the workplace. Instead, create realistic goals for yourself that you will be likely be able to meet.

A good part of knowing that there is only a limited amount of time in the day and a limited number of things for you to do is also knowing when to say "no." Although you may not always have the pleasure of telling someone no in the workplace, you should have more flexibility at home. If you can't afford to take on extra assignments at work, don't. If you can't find the time to complete another task at home, like dust or vacuum, seek help from your partner, your children, or a professional housecleaner.

In addition to creating a goal list, it is also advised that you create a to-do-list for yourself. Depending on how out of sync you are with your time, a daily to-do-list may be required. After time, you may be able to graduate to a weekly or even monthly to do list.

When creating your list, it is important to know the importance of prioritizing. First, it is important to determine which tasks are the most important. What tasks have the greatest sense of urgency? Those are ones that should be at the top of your list.

As for ease, an easy way to improve your sense of time management is to eliminate or limit your distractions. If you find yourself wasting a considerable of time, what is it that distracts you or gets you off task? Is it the internet, socializing with friends, or the television?

If the above mentioned approaches still aren't able to help you manage your time like you had hoped, you may want to consider hiring the services of a professional. As previously stated, if you need additional help at home you may want to hire a professional housecleaner. With that said, did you also know that there are experts who can show you how to better manage and make use of your time, as well as those who can help you get your home or office more organized? There are. The professional help, knowledge, and expertise of these individuals is never a bad thing.

Chapter 8: Personal Time Management Tips

Are you an individual who just feels as if you can never catch up? Do you feel like you can't get everything that you need to do done? If so, it is important that you take steps to rectify the problem. Poor time management is often associated with the workplace, but did you know that your personal life can be negatively impacted as well? It can be.

As for how poor time management can have a negative impact on your personal life, you may be surprised just what it can do. For example, if you have a poor sense of time you may find that your relationship with your spouse, romantic partner, friends, or children suffers. Those who have a poor sense of time are often stressed, frustrated, and unorganized. This is likely to put a significant strain on otherwise healthy relationships.

Despite the fact that time management can have a negative impact on your personal life, there is good news. That good news is that there are ways that you can prevent your poor use of time from becoming too much of a problem. The biggest way to prevent this from happening involves learning how to make better use of your time. To help you get started, a number of personal time management tips are outlined below.

An easy way to learn how to make better use of your time involves creating and relying on to do lists. If you have everyday tasks that have become a part of your routine, like getting your kids ready for school or going to work, you do not necessarily have to include these items on your list. With that said, other non-daily tasks should be added. These tasks may include running an errand before work, attending a child's sporting event, helping your child with an important school project, going on a date, and so forth.

Learning how to prioritize is another important component of being able to properly manage your time. It is important to remember that the day and its time is limited. If you have a family and a fulltime job, you may find it difficult or downright impossible to get everything done. If that is the case, be sure to prioritize. You can leave the lesser important tasks, such as dusting your house as opposed to doing laundry for later or the following day.

The use of time management tools is another easy way that you can go about making better use of your time. There are a number of tools that you can use to your advantage. A to do list was sited as an example above. Other tools that you may be able to benefit from the use of include alarm clocks and daily or weekly planners. Since most time management tools are affordable, already in your home, or free to create, you should use them to your advantage.

One of the many reasons why people end up wasting time is because they are easily distracted. If you feel this is the main source of your time management problems, you will want to determine what your biggest distractions are. For example, do you spend too much time socializing with coworkers after work or with the neighbours? If so, you don't have to completely eliminate this contact, but try to limit it. The same can be said with television and internet use.

Chapter 9: Successful Time Management Techniques

Are you an individual who finds it difficult to manage your time at work or at home or at both places? If you are, you may be looking for information on how you can make better use of your time. You will likely be pleased with all of your options, as there are a number of different steps that you can take. A few successful time management techniques that have worked for others, just like you, are touched on below.

One of the most successful time management techniques is that of goal setting. Goals provide many with an important source of needed motivation, as they give you something to specifically aim for. Whether you set a long-term goal, such as improving the management of your time in general, or a short-term goal, such as showing up for work on time, goals are important. However, make sure that the time management goals you do set for yourself are realistic. Creating daily to do lists is another one of the many ways that you can go about making better use of your time. In fact, after time has passed, you may not even need to use a daily to do list. For the time being, a to do list can help make sure that you stay focused and on task. It can also help create a new routine for yourself, one where you are better aware of your time and what must be done.

In addition to creating a simple to do list, you are also urged to prioritize. In fact, prioritizing combined with daily to do lists is the best form of time management. Whether your to do list is for the home or work, take a close look at all of the tasks you need to complete. Which tasks are more important? To reduce stress, add those with the most urgency to the top of your to do list.

Another successful time management technique is one that is very easy, but many people have a hard time doing it. This time management technique is just saying no. It is important to remember that there are only a limited number of hours in the day. No matter how much time and effort you put into staying focused and on task, there are still some things that you may not get accomplished. That is why you should never take on more than you reasonably believe that you can handle.

If you do find yourself saying yes to completing an extra project at work or taking on too many responsibilities at home, it is important to remember that you can ask for help. In fact, knowing when to ask for help is an important component of time management. You can ask your friends, children, or romantic partner for help around the house. You may also want to call upon the services of a professional housecleaner. In the workplace, consider outsourcing your work to another employee, if you are able to do so without getting into trouble.

Staying organized is another easy, yet effective and successful time management technique. In fact, did you know that time management and organization go hand in hand? They do. If you are organized, you will spend less time searching for lost or misplaced items or other important work documents. The more organized you are at both home and work, the easier it will be for you to manage your time.

Chapter 10: The Danger of Not Managing Your Time at the Office

Are you employed? If you are and if you work in an office setting, do you know how to make good use of your time? If not, it is vital to your success and your financial standings that you start doing so as soon as possible.

Unfortunately, many individuals do not know the many consequences that they may face if they don't perform their best at work. Even if you have been able to slide under the radar before socializing with coworkers or surfing the internet, your time of just messing around may soon come to an end. This is because more employers realize just how much money they are truly losing with employees who don't know how to manage their time.

As for the dangers of not properly managing your time at work, you are less likely to stay focused and on task. If you do not understand the importance of managing your time at work, you are more likely to get distracted, which may delay an important project or prevent you from meeting a deadline. This, in itself, can have a number of serious consequences. In a professional workplace, you shouldn't miss a deadline unless you have a good reason for doing so.

Another danger of not managing your time is that you are likely to get unorganized easily. In fact, did you know that organization and time management go hand in hand? If you do not know how to properly manage your time, you likely rush to complete simple tasks, such as putting away important files. This will likely result in errors. However, when you later go to find those important files or documents, they may not be where you thought. This may result in you wasting time searching for them.

Although you may not necessarily think about this danger, it is still important to take into consideration. That danger is setting a bad example. Many individuals do not understand the ripple effect that most workplaces have. If other co-workers see that you are able to waste your time, either by socializing or playing computer games, they may try to do the same, especially if you are able to get away with this type of behaviour. You may unintentionally endanger a whole office or company.

Perhaps, the biggest danger of not knowing how to properly manage your time at the workplace is putting your job at risk. As previously stated, many business owners are realizing just how much money they are losing on poor performing employees; therefore, many are starting to take action. You may receive a warning first, but there is a good chance that you will lose your job. After all, why should a company pay you to not work when there are hundreds of other men and women out there who would love to have your job?

If the possibility of losing your job wasn't enough, it is important to take into consideration what can and will likely happen with your good name. If you are terminated from your job, chances are you will find it difficult to find a job in a similar position. This is most often the case if you had a good, well paying job, such as that of an office manager. Many high paying positions require recommendations and job references. If you get terminated from your position, these will be hard to come by. In fact, instead of not giving any comment at all, you may end up getting a bad recommendation!

The above mentioned examples are just a few of the many ways that you may end up suffering from poor productivity at work. The good news, however, is that you may be surprised just how easy it is to change your ways. Whether you choose to create daily to do lists for yourself, use a computerized day planner, or learn to better prioritize your responsibilities, get started with doing so as soon as possible.

Chapter 11: The Importance of Personal Time Management

Are you an individual who knows how to make good use of your time? If you are not, you may want to learn ways to make improvements. This is because time management can have a negative impact on your personal life. Unfortunately, many individuals only believe that poor time management hurts those in the workplace, but this isn't the case. In fact, there are a number of ways that your personal life can suffer from poor time management.

If you do not know how to manage your time, there is a good chance that you will be stressed out. You may also feel a wide range of other emotions, including anger, frustration, and fear. With that said, if you know how to properly manage time you are more likely to live a happy, healthy, productive, and stress free life.

Although we often associate poor time management with missed deadlines and showing up late to work, it is important to remember that the same can be said with your social life. Do you have friends? How much do you stay in contact with them? How often do you get together for coffee or lunch? If you do, do you show up for your meetings with friends late or do you forget to make regular contact with them? If you do, you may end up putting your friendships at risk.

In addition to having a negative impact on your friendships, poor time management may also have an impact on your relationship. To have a healthy and happy relationship, time management is important. You need to know how much time you should devote to your spouse, as opposed to spending it working, watching television, or hanging out with friends.

Time management is also important as you want to make sure that you arrive home or at dates on time.
If you are a parent, having poor time management may also impact the relationship that you have with your children. When you are a parent, you have responsibilities to your children. The most common of these responsibilities is to feed and clothe your children. Depending on their ages, you may also be reasonable for getting them ready and sent off to school or daycare. If you do not have proper sense of time or if you do just choose not to use your time wisely, you can end up hurting your children, like by making them late to school or other important events. All individuals are encouraged to have good sense of time, but it is vital for parents.

In keeping with being a parent, if you are a parent, poor use of your time also sets bad examples for your children. Whether your children are teenagers, toddlers, or elementary school aged, they will likely make note of your behaviours. If you want your children to get good grades at school and later get good jobs, it is important that you teach them all about time management and its importance. One of the best ways to do so is by setting a good example for your children. The good news is that this is a lot easier than it sounds. You can set a good example for your children by getting ready for work in the morning on time or by arriving at scheduled events on time.

Another one of the many ways that having a poor sense of time management can hurt you is with your credit. Those who have poor time management also often have poor credit. This is because those who are unable to properly manage their time often pay their bills late. With credit cards, this can result in expensive minimum payments that just cannot be paid. By knowing when all of your bills are due, you are likely to have better credit, but time management is important.

As you can see, there are a number of ways that poor time management can negatively impact your personal life. For that reason, take steps to make sure it doesn't impact yours.

Chapter 12: Time Management Tips to Help you See Success

Are you a person who finds it difficult to stay focused and to stay on task? Are you regularly late for important events or do you turn in projects or homework after the deadline? If you do, you may need to improve your time management. The good news is that there are a number of tips that can help you do so. A few of these tips are outlined below for your convenience.

One of the first things that you will want to do is create time management goals for yourself. These goals can be for different things. For example, you can set a main goal of improving your time management in a specific period of time, like two weeks or a month. You can also set individual goals for yourself, like arriving to parties, social events, work, or important business meetings on time. No matter what goals you choose to set for yourself, they are important, as goals work to provide motivation.

Another way to improve your time management is to determine where you have the most problems. What exactly is it that causes you to waste time? Chances are you already know. If not, do a little test. Walk though a normal day and record what times you get distracted the most and what you are doing at those times. Do you find yourself wasting time when socializing with friends, using the internet, or watching television? If so, reduce or completely eliminate those distractions.

As previously stated, a to do list is a time management tool that you can benefit from using. As helpful as a to do list can be, it is important to also prioritize. You will want to list your items in order of importance. For example, if your list focuses on tasks to do at home is it more important for you to do laundry, vacuum the house, or wash dishes? The order of your lists should all depend on importance and urgency.

One of the best ways to properly manage your time is to stay organized. In fact, poor organization is the leading cause of wasted time. If you are employed, be sure to keep your office desk clean and clutter free. When doing so, you are able to stay focused and on task better. You should be able to get more work done, as you should spend less time searching for misplaced or lost documents. Organization is not only important in the workplace, but other areas that you frequent, such as your home or your car.

The above mentioned time management tips should be able to help you better manage your time on your own. With that said, it is important to remember that sometimes help is needed. The last thing that you want to do is be overloaded, whether it be at work or at home. If you need to outsource some of your work to a co-worker or if you need to hire the services of a professional housecleaner, go ahead and do so. Once you are caught back up, you can begin to properly manage your time. As much as we all want to complete our responsibilities on our own, it is important to remember that sometimes help is needed.

By taking the above mentioned points into consideration, you may be able to better improve the use of your time. There are a number of benefits to having effective time management both at home and at the workplace.

Chapter 13: Time Management Training: What It Entails

Are you a Company Senior executive, a business owner or head of government? If you are, you must know the importance of time management in the office. Did you know that when your employees don't know how to manage their time, they likely end up costing your organisation money? Whether you are a senior executive, a business owner or head of government, you do not want to see this happen.

When it comes to poor time management at the office, there are many senior executive, business owner and head of government who choose to provide their employees with time management training. If this sounds like a good idea to you, you may be looking for more information. You may be curious as to exactly what time management training it's, how it works, and what your staff members will learn. If these are all questions that you have, you will want to continue reading on.

When understanding time management training, it is important to remember that it does come in a number of different formats. For example, most companies choose to hire outside specialists. These are individuals or teams of individuals who come in and teach staff members the importance of proper time management, as well as share tips on how to get the most done through the day. A good example of this is by showing or helping your staff members get their office desks better organized. This is key, as organization and time management go hand in hand.

As nice as it is to hire outside help from professional office organizers and time management specialists, the cost of doing so may be a put off for you. If it is, you may be able to host your own time management training sessions. Doing so is actually a lot easier than you may originally think. In fact, many business owners and office managers like this approach as it gives them complete control over what their staff members learn.

Speaking of what your staff members will likely learn in time management training will vary. As previously stated, you can hire outside help or you can perform your own training sessions. Regardless of which approach you do take, there are some things that you will want to make sure that your staff members know. First, make sure that you not only tell them the importance of properly managing their time at the office, but show them ways that they can improve the use of their time. These ways may involve keeping a clean and organized office desk, completing a to do list each morning, and so forth.

It is also important that you outline the consequences for employees who continue to waste company time. After time management training has been offered to all employees, there is no reason why employees should be seen standing around, socializing with each other, or using an office computer for personal use. State that these things are okay for break time, but not during normal work hours. You may want to go as far to show your staff members just how much their wasted time is costing the company. Let them know that additional warnings may come, with termination being a possibility.

As a reminder, time management training is not required by many means, but you may find it a relatively easy and effective approach, especially when compared to terminating and rehiring new employees.

Chapter 14: The Pros and Cons of Time Management Training in the Workplace

Are you head of government, a business owner or senior executive? If you are, time management should be of great importance to you. If your employees do not know how to make proper use of their time, you could be suffering the consequences. As for what those consequences are, they may include the loss of profits and a poor public perception.

If and when you determine that your employees are wasting their workday or even just a few minutes here and there, you will want to take action. In fact, the sooner that you take action, the better it will be for you and your company. As for what action you should take, you may want to consider time management training.

Time management training; it sounds professional and effective, but what is it? In all honesty, you will find that time management training comes in a number of different formats. For starters, you can have you own time management training run by you and your staff. On the other hand, you can use the assistance of a professional. There are individuals who specialize in teaching others how to stay organized, focused, and on task. You can hire one of these individuals to come into your workplace and educate your employees.

Now that you know what your main options are in terms of time management training for your office, you may be curious as to what the pros and cons are. For starters, the cost can be quite high. Many professionals charge a set rate, but others charge depending on the number of guests in attendance. One way that you can keep your cost down is by only requiring your problem workers to seek training. Another way is by hosting your own training sessions. This should be relatively cost effective for you.

Another con or downside to time management training in the workplace is the time that you must spend doing the trainings. In a way, it can seem like you are wasting the time of your company. In some instances it may be a time waste, but it is important for you to remember the end result. Taking an hour or even two hours to teach your staff the importance of time management, as well as sharing tips on how to be productive in the workplace is likely worth the time spent.

Although there are a number of cons or downsides to having your staff members sit through time management training, there are also a number of pros or plus sides to doing so as well. One of those is the fact that you are able to provide your staff members with a refresher course in the area of time management. This is a nice alternative to terminating some of your employees. In fact, some of your best performing employees may have problems managing their time. What this means is that when they actually do choose to work, they are likely to produce the best results. These are the type of employees that you will want to work with, not terminate right away.

Another one of the many pros or plus sides to having your staff members undergo time management training is that they shouldn't have any excuses. When you or a professional lays out specific ways that your employees can better manage their time at work, they don't have any excuses for not doing so. They can't claim that they didn't know that there were specific approaches they could take, as they sat through the meeting or training session. In fact, once your employees go through a training session, they are likely to know that they are being watched. This alone should reduce the amount of time that is wasted by your employees and produce better results.

Since there are a number of both pros and cons to offering time management training to your staff member, you need to decide if it is right for you and your organisation. If you are noticing a lot of staff members who take too long to complete their work or if you just see your employees hanging around the office, time management training is a good idea.

Chapter 15: What to Do With Employees Who Do Not Properly Manage Their Time

Are you a head of government, a business owner or senior executive? If you are, there is a good chance that you have employees in your staff who does not know how to manage their time. What do you do with these employees? If you are unsure as to how you should proceed, please continue reading on.

First, it is important to do something. The last thing that you will want to do is let an employee who has bad time management fly under the radar. Many business owners do not think about this at the time, but there are serious consequences for not calling out poor performing workers.

One of the many consequences to allowing one of your employees to keep on wasting their time and yours is that others are likely to follow suit. Even some of your best performing employees are likely to waste time socially or by surfing the internet when they see that others are able to do the same and get away with it.

Your business profits will also likely be put at risk. When an employee spends too much time surfing the internet or wasting time in general, it will likely take much longer for you to get projects completed. This can have an impact on your business profits. For example, you may later end up paying your employee overtime to complete a task that they should have finished during normal work hours.

If your business deals directly with the general public, an employee who does not know how to manage their time can also have a negative impact on your company's public perception. Deadlines should not be missed, but proper time management is vital when working with clients. Did you agree to have forms drawn up on time for a client of yours? If you did, they should be ready when expected. If not, your client may look elsewhere. Also, places that have employees just hanging around the office and socializing tends to look unprofessional in nature.

So, you now know the consequences of letting an employee with poor time management slide, but what should you do?

It is important to bring a lack of time management to the attention of your employee or employees. Let them know that wasting time on the clock is not acceptable, especially when there are other tasks or projects that they could be working on. Clearly state that socializing is for break times only.

Next, be sure not to let the same behaviour continue. Workers who have been warned about wasting their time and the time of the company should not have any excuse for doing so. Give one more final warning before taking evasive action. This action may include terminating your employee's position with the company.

Despite the fact that termination is an option, you may have what you believe to be an otherwise good employee. If that is the case, you may want to opt for time management training. This can be done yourself or with the services of a third party. In fact, if you have a large number of employees who seem to not know how to manage their time, you may want to opt for companywide training.

Should you decide to host your own time management training seminar, as opposed to using outside help, be sure to share tips with your employees, outline the importance of making good use of their time at the workplace, as well as the consequences of not doing so. This leaves no room for exceptions and you should see a significant improvement in productivity in your workplace.

As a recap, if you are a business owner or even just an office manager, it is important to make sure that all of your employees are working to the best of their ability. Your company and your own personal reputation may end up taking the fall for those who do not perform to the best of their ability.

Chapter 16: 101 Ways to Get More Done With Less Stress

1: Identify the activities in your day that are time-stealers

Keep track of how much time you spend reading emails, browsing the web and chatting on the telephone because these are some of the most well known time-stealers. After you track the time that you spend on these activities, it is likely that you will automatically start to decrease your time-stealing activities.

2: Start by setting achievable goals

Even the smallest goals can put you on the track to better time management skills. Set a small goal, like not reading personal emails during work hours for a week or filing your mail the day it comes in instead of letting it pile up. Once you've achieved this small goal, move on to something bigger. Before you know it your time management issues will be a thing of the past.

3: Set up a plan for time management

Why? Well, quite simply your efforts to better manage your time will not be noticeable until you start keeping track of the progress that you are making. Create a simple chart and put it on your desk or refrigerator – somewhere where you'll see it every day; then fill out what you plan to do and when you did it. This will help you see at a glance what needs to be done and as you complete items you'll feel a sense of accomplishment.

4: Find a time management system that works for you

Some sort of time management tool is crucial for making your time management goals a reality. Whether it's a computer program, a PDA, a wall calendar, a desk calendar, or something else, the key is to find something you like and use it. But be sure to keep only one. Having different systems for work and home only leads to confusion.

5: Use the reminder option in your online calendar

Whether you use an online calendar, the calendar with your email software or even your mobile phone – use the reminder feature because it will help you to remember what you have planned for a specific block of time.

6: Spend a few moments each morning looking over your task list

Decide first what you need to do during the coming day. Then, rank the items that absolutely must be done in terms of priority. It is important to do this every morning to get into the habit of prioritizing. Studies show that you must do something 21 times to make it a habit. So stick with it and within a few weeks you'll find you do this automatically each morning.

7: Delegate whenever possible

If you need to pick up dry cleaning, fill your petrol tank and stop at the grocery store on the way from work consider asking your spouse to take some of the load for you. Asking for a little help sometimes can save your sanity and free up time in your schedule to help things run more smoothly.

8: Start a routine and stick to a schedule

Routine and schedule – two words that most people hate – are the two most important words when it comes to effective time management. You need to establish a routine and a schedule, and you need to work hard to stick to them as much as possible. Do yourself a favour and get your entire family involved. If everyone is aware of what they're expected to do and when, things will run a lot smoother.

9: Don't waste time waiting

One of the largest time wasters that people complain about is waiting. Instead of just waiting before your next doctor's appointment or while the oil is being changed in your car, take along your task list for the following day or your cheque book if it needs balancing.

10: Understand what good time management really is

Time management means more than just keeping track of how you spend your time – it means finding ways to change your routine to get more out of the time you have during the day. Time management is not simply rearranging your schedule in order to fit in as much as possible. It means taking care not to over-schedule your day whenever possible. Balance is the key to getting the important things done, while still finding time to enjoy life!

11: Never allow work to interfere with your downtime

Whether your downtime is an entire weekend, an hour in the morning to work out or a few hours for TV watching in the evening, that time is necessary for you to recharge and energize yourself so that you can be more effective. Block this leisure time off in your calendar and honour it the same way you do your other commitments.

12: Set a time each day for uninterrupted work

Whatever it is you have to work on, make it a priority to have some time every day for uninterrupted work. If this is unrealistic for you, at least try to minimize interruptions as much as possible by turning off the ringer on your phone and putting up a do not disturb sign for a few hours each day. This time will allow you to focus on getting things done and the sense of accomplishment will help you be more productive for the rest of the day.

13: Keep track of your daily activities

For one week, carry a notebook and write down everything that you do during the course of a day. This is very helpful, because it will allow you to determine a benchmark for where your time management efforts will begin. From this information look for obvious time wasters like running to the grocery store several times a week for forgotten items, or spending 10 minutes every morning searching for your car keys. When you see how your time is really spent you will be able to identify areas that can be improved.

14: Talk to other people who are working on developing their time management skills

Almost everyone struggles with effectively managing their time. Find a friend or co-worker who is also working on this and talk about your downfalls, achievements and discoveries. Just like anything else, having a support network is an excellent way to improve your chances of success.

15: Determine what is most important

If you are working on time management at work, which functions of your position are the most critical? If you are working on time management at home, which responsibilities are the most important to the running of your household? Put together a list of what your priorities are so that if something needs to be cut it is an easy decision to make.

16: Never ask yourself if you feel like doing something

We all face things in life that we do not feel like doing, and if we spent less time not wanting to do them and more time actually getting them done, think about how much more productive we could be! So next time you find yourself having a conversation in your head about not wanting to do something, just get it done and make it a habit.

17: Find your peak performance time

Everyone has a different time during the day when they are the most efficient. Pay attention to when you are able to get the most done and then be sure you are using that time for your most important tasks. If you are more effective in the morning, make every attempt to get into the office early. Or, if you find that evening is your best time of day, it might be a good idea to work a later shift if possible.

18: Touch a piece of paper only once

A great time management trick is to touch a piece of paper only one time. Make a decision the first time you read it to either file it or throw it away. If you do this, you will notice immediately that the time you spend reviewing piles of paper is significantly decreased.

19: Be flexible with yourself

If you find that your schedule is overloaded, be realistic and willingly accept that you sometimes cannot get everything finished in one day. You'll accomplish nothing by beating yourself up over it. Instead take some time to figure out why you are so busy and look for ways to eliminate some items from your to-do list. Are you always the one driving the kids to football practice? Ask another parent to help. Do you spend hours cleaning after everyone else is in bed? Assign chores and get the whole family to pitch in. And don't forget that sometimes it's alright to give yourself a break and leave some things to be done another day.

20: Don't forget about time for yourself

Make sure that you schedule personal time for yourself at some point every day. Even if you are only able to fit in a few minutes, don't skip this important appointment with yourself. Use it to take a walk, have a bubble bath or watch your favourite television program. Don't look at this as time wasted. Instead remember that by taking a little while to recharge your batteries you will be more efficient at the other tasks you have to complete.

21: Don't let technology become a hindrance instead of a help

If you use a PDA, learn how to USE the PDA. Sometimes, people change over to a PDA and find themselves spending more time trying to figure out how to use the calendar than they do getting their task list finished. The same holds true for fancy computerized calendars. Sometimes a plain old paper and pen is best!

22: Keep your email inbox in order

When you read an email make a decision about what to do with it immediately. If it is spam, delete it. If you have replied to it and it does not need to be saved then delete it. And if it's important file it right away. Don't leave it sitting in your inbox until you have hundreds of them to go through. This waste time unnecessarily and can be a source of anxiety knowing that such a large task is looming.

23: Learn how to use your email program's spam filters

People today spend more time than ever filtering through their email to determine what is spam and what is actually legitimate email. Spam filters can save you a few minutes every day that you can spend on other things.

24: Have more than one task list

Instead of one large to-do list, opt for separate lists for work and home, and separate your lists into individual lists for projects and tasks. This way, your task list seems a lot more manageable and less cluttered. Studies show that if you look at your list and see 25 things to be done, you'll feel overwhelmed and be less likely to do any of them.

25: Distinguish between small projects and large projects

Realize that large projects may require many tasks to complete, and that small projects like getting a haircut may take just one step. Keep track of the tasks associated with every project that you need to accomplish. By breaking out your large projects into manageable tasks you can see progress being made.

26: Use the ABC prioritization method

"A" projects are those that are important because they will contribute to your long-term success. "B" projects are important but not urgent. And "C" projects are the ones it would be nice to get to if you have time. Always start with any "A" tasks and break them down into smaller, easier to handle tasks so you can accomplish them quicker. Then move on to "B" tasks and finally – if there is time – the "C" tasks.

27: Weigh tasks according to both urgency and importance

Not sure how to start prioritizing everything you have to get done? Look at each task and determine how urgent it is, and how important it is. Although something is important, it may not be urgent. And, just because something is not important does not mean that it is not urgent (or time sensitive). The most logical place to start is with tasks that are both urgent and important.

28: Don't let negative emotions stop you from completing a task

If you find that negative emotions are keeping you from completing a task, spend some time trying to determine the cause and figure out what you can do to alleviate the feelings so that you can move forward with what needs to be done.

29: Listen to self-improvement audio books

There are lots of different books now available in mp3 format so you can listen to them during your commute, while you workout or even while you're running errands. Look for ones that can help give you new tips and techniques for better time management. Although you may not be consciously listening 100% of the time, you will pick up tips that can help to make your time management skills better.

30: Get organized!

Studies have shown that people who are organized spend less time looking for important items and more time completing the tasks on their to-do list. So buy some filing cabinets, mail sorters, drawer organizers or whatever other organization aids you need for your home and office. It may be a big task to find a new home for everything but once it's done you'll be amazed at the time you can save!

31: Learn to identify things that are a waste of your time

Some things to look out for include: a failure to plan properly, stress, fatigue, meetings without a clear agenda, clerical tasks at work that could be effectively delegated and unplanned interruptions. Once you identify these time wasters you can work to avoid them or better manage them in the future.

32: Set meeting agendas

This way everyone in attendance will know ahead of time what is to be discussed and what the intended outcome of the meeting is to be. Even if the meeting is just a simple brainstorming session, it is best to announce this ahead of time so that everyone is on the same page.

33: Set up timelines for group projects

When you have more than just yourself to manage, it is critical that everyone know their role and responsibilities when it comes to project completion. This way, you will spend more time working and less time explaining what everyone should be doing and when.

34: Define your goals and priorities each week

Goals and priorities change. What is important today may no longer be a top priority next week, so you need to be willing to shift your focus occasionally. By evaluating what is important to you on a regular basis you will ensure that you are always focusing your time on the most important tasks.

35: Clean off your desk

At work or at home, one of the number one time wasters is a desk with more than 20% of the surface covered. Clear your desk and you will see an immediate improvement in your productivity.

36: Don't procrastinate

If you see something that needs done, do it now instead of spending a lot of time thinking about why it needs done and why you haven't already done it. In the time you would take thinking about it and rescheduling it you could have it completed and out of the way.

37: Learn how to say "no"

If someone asks you to fit just one more thing into your schedule, or to do something that you can't or don't want to do – say no. You may find this difficult in the beginning but it will get easier as you start to see the benefits.

38: Limit the number of meetings you attend

Meetings at work are often a huge time waster. Therefore, make every attempt to reduce the amount of meetings that you attend. Possibly delegate attendance to someone else, or just ask for a copy of the minutes when your input is not as importance as the follow-up activities.

39: Have a long-term goal

One large overall goal will help you to develop short-term smaller goals that can be more easily achieved. Having an end point in mind is important when planning your time. Simply break your larger goals into smaller, more manageable tasks.

40: Build time management related goals into your schedule

For example, include on your to-do-list that you will spend 15 minutes at the end of every day to get organized for the next day. By making time management a priority you will find that it soon becomes less of a chore and more of a habit.

41: End each day ready to start the next

At the end of every work day, make sure that your desk is cleaned off and that you have at least started a task list for the following day. This will make your next morning smoother, and allow you to get started as soon as you get in.

42: Don't waste time on the telephone

Telephone calls are a big time waster for many people. Try to minimize this problem by planning the calls that you need to make ahead of time and then making several calls in a row instead of spreading them throughout the day. Try to set a time limit for each call, and stick to it as closely as you can. Often letting the person you are calling know upfront that it will be a quick call is all it takes. Simply start by saying "I only have a few minutes to talk... "Or "This is just a quick call to let you know about...".

43: Determine the times during the day when you are least effective

Everyone has downtimes it's only natural. By recognizing when yours are you can plan your lunch or and other break times during those less efficient periods. Often a break is all it takes to help you clear your mind so you can return to the task at hand more focused.

44: Minimize stress by getting small tasks out of the way

Stress usually arises because of the list of things you still need to do, and not because of the things that you have already done. Help minimize stress by quickly completing the easiest tasks on your list. Once you have a momentum going you will be about to tackle larger, more involved tasks.

45: Stop wasting time looking for things

Many people spend a lot of unnecessary time each day looking for things. By better organizing your home or workspace you will know exactly where things are instead of having to hunt for them. This will free up more time to work on the tasks that you need to get done. Certainly, getting organized can take a while initially – but once you get in the habit life will be easier.

46: Keep an organized filing cabinet

At least once a month, review your filing cabinets to make sure your files are organized in the most effective manner for your habits and that they contain useful and complete information. Remove old paperwork and items that simply do not belong. This will make it quicker and easier for you to find what you need when you need it instead of sorting through irrelevant files and useless papers.

47: Organize your paperwork

If you find your file folders are bursting with papers, it is time to implement a new filing strategy. Try colour coding your files so they are easy to find. Or start sub file folders. Simply use a large divider file to hold individual sub-files in order to keep everything together. Keeping your paperwork organized will reduce the amount of time that you spend looking for specific items.

48: Ask yourself "is this an effective use of my time?"

Doing so may remind you that there are other priorities that you should be addressing instead of what you are currently doing.

49: Set realistic timelines to complete projects

When working with a timeline, try to identify early on where you think problems might occur. Building in some padding is a good idea where you see potential problems arising. If everything goes smoothly, you will finish ahead of time. If there is a problem, you will be better equipped to resolve it and still finish when expected.

50: Be proactive with your planning

Do you tend to leave things until the last minute? You are not alone! But remember that the more you plan to get things done ahead of time, the better off you will be. If you are proactive about making tasks a priority a couple of days before they need to be completed, you will be more effective and a lot less stressed.

51: Eliminate distractions so you can focus

If you are the type of person who is easily distracted by your surroundings, consider finding a quiet place to work so that you can more effectively use your time. You might also want to try wearing headphones, which can minimize distractions like background noise, television or the telephone.

52: Keep a list of events in chronological order so you know what is coming up

Whenever possible, keep a list of your weekly appointments, meetings and social obligations in chronological order. A good calendar software program or even a spreadsheet program can help you to sort and re-order your list as required. Doing so will help you always know what is coming up next so you can plan your schedule accordingly. If there is a birthday party on Saturday you will know at a glance and can remember to pick up a gift next time you are out running errands instead of waiting until the last minute.

53: Break large tasks into smaller, more manageable ones

Large tasks are daunting; therefore it is a great idea to break large tasks into more manageable pieces, which can be done over time instead of all at once. This is a great tip, particularly for those who tend to procrastinate.

54: Reward yourself for your achievements

There is nothing more encouraging than receiving a reward for meeting a goal, even when you provide the reward! For example, after you have finished cleaning out your closet, take a break to watch your favorite television show. Or if you stick to your time management goals for an entire week, treat yourself to that new pair of shoes you have been wanting. If you have something to work toward it can be the extra incentive you need to get things done.

55: Use the 90-second rule

Using the 90 second rule you will get into the habit of spending no more than 90 seconds deciding whether or not to keep a piece of paperwork, fix a small problem, prevent a potential problem or make a short-term decision. This gets the small tasks that pop up unexpectedly out of the way instead of letting them build into a huge task.

56: Come up with a plan to manage housework

Do you let the housework pile up until it becomes a huge task? A full day of cleaning is daunting and many people tend to let things go for a few weeks because they can't decide where to start. Instead, make it a habit to do 2 or 3 small tasks every day. The 15 or so minutes that you spend will save you countless hours in the long run.

57: Try this method of organizing your time

The next time you are planning out your day, make a large square on the paper, and divide into four smaller squares. The top left is for things that are both important and time sensitive. The top right is for things that are not important, but are time sensitive. The bottom left is for things that are important but not time sensitive. The bottom right is for things that are not important and not time sensitive.

58: Buy back a little of your time

If you are always short on time, it may be a good idea to hire someone to help you with things like housekeeping, lawn care, grocery shopping or even to lend a hand around the office. This will free up your time for the more important tasks on your to-do-list. Or give you a much deserved break!

59: Only check your voicemail once a day

How many times each day do you check your voicemail? Determine at what point in the day checking messages would be most effective and try only checking your voicemail once each day for a week. And when you do check it, take action on the calls you received rather than letting them pile up. This simple change can potentially save you 10 or 15 minutes a day.

60: Don't allow interruptions to throw you off course

If you receive a telephone call at a busy time, ask the caller if it would be ok for you to return their call in an hour, when you are finished with the task at hand. Make a note, and remember to call back when you said that you would.

61: Make record keeping quick and easy

Something you can do to make record keeping easier for yourself is to pick a time each week when you will empty your wallet of the week's receipts. At that time, file them appropriately. Not only will you save yourself the time required to empty your wallet after it is bursting with papers, but when it's time to do your taxes you will have everything you need, all together in the right place.

62: Be careful that you don't overlook important tasks because you're short for time

If you decide to remove some tasks from your routine, be sure that you do not eliminate important tasks such as balancing your cheque book or comparing your receipts with your credit card bill. These tasks are often overlooked when people are trying to save time, and they can definitely cost you money in the long run.

63: Prepare at night, for what you will do in the morning

If you find yourself wasting a lot of time looking for your car keys, wallet and other essentials it is a good idea to develop a habit of always putting your things in one place - the SAME place - every night before you go to bed. In the morning when you're rushed it can mean the difference between starting off on a good note and starting off with a headache!

64: Set your alarm clock 15 minutes earlier in order to give yourself more time in the morning

This will give you time to fit in breakfast, if you normally skip it. It will also give you more than the time you need to sit down and prioritize what is on your to-do list for the day.

65: Identify the top three items on your priority list for each day

Put those at the top of the list. Do everything you can to scratch off those three tasks every day, and you will find that you are actually getting more done, because you will feel as though you are accomplishing a great deal, just by knocking out the three most important things.

66: Choose your hobbies carefully

Hobbies are important; however in most cases they also require a significant time commitment. If you are considering taking up a new hobby, determine one or two other hobbies that no longer keep your interest. Consider a trade off, and you will have more time to devote to your new hobby.

67: Consolidate your technology devices

Do you have a cell phone? A PDA? A Laptop? Are you TOO connected? Consider consolidating your data onto one device that you can carry with you, and spend less time trying to synch your data from one device to all of the others.

68: Create checklists for complicated tasks that you do frequently

For example, if you frequently travel for work or pleasure, keep a checklist handy of the things you need to do before you leave. If you have a set of identification cards that you need to have with you keep them together and in a specific location. Include on the list reminders to have your mail held, paper delivery stopped or even to phone the neighbours to let them know that you will be gone and for how long.

69: Get an answering machine

Are calls constantly taking your focus away from what you are doing? An answering machine might be an investment worth making so that your meals go uninterrupted, and so that you can avoid the constant interruptions of your time.

70: Create an action list

If you frequently attend meetings, conferences or other activities where you gather notes and information, plan to immediately review those documents and make yourself an action list of things that you will do in response to the recent activity. Go through documents, brochures and other paperwork that you received and keep only what is important.

71: Try to consolidate errands as much as possible

For example, unless it's an emergency don't go to the hardware store for only one thing. The same can apply to the post office, the library, the grocery store and the dry cleaners. We all experience times when a single purpose errand cannot be avoided, but you can save a tremendous amount of time if you put together several errands per trip. Simply keep a list of everything that is waiting to be done so nothing is forgotten.

72: Check your email at set times during the day

Set a few specific times, like first thing in the morning, after lunch and right before you leave for the day to check your work email. Try to avoid checking personal email more than once a day and send responses immediately to all emails whenever possible. Not only will you have less email to get through later but you also won't forget to answer an important email.

73: When sending an email, always use an appropriate subject

Most people simply hit the reply button when responding but doing so can make it difficult to find that email later. Especially if several emails go back and forth! Instead include an appropriate subject so you know what the email contains.

74: Don't allow yourself to procrastinate

Everyone occasionally procrastinates to avoid doing tasks that are not enjoyable, but when you have something that simply cannot wait, just get it done. For one thing, it's off of your task list and for another thing, you won't be spending a lot of unnecessary time thinking about what you need to be doing.

75: Record "pending" tasks in your calendar

These are items that will not happen until sometime in the future, or cannot happen until someone else has done a particular action. Mark down these items in your calendar so that you have a reminder to check the progress, or to include the task on an upcoming to-do-list.

76: Don't give yourself too much time to complete tasks

There is an old saying that "any task or project can swell to take up the amount of time that you have dedicated to its completion". This is definitely true. A good plan is to reduce the amount of time that you allot to a specific task, until you find the right amount of time. Sometimes, this may not work out as expected but in most cases you will find some extra time in your schedule as a result.

77: Try to get the most dreaded item on your task list out of the way as early in the day as possible

This way, you won't spend the day trying to avoid doing it and thinking about it. And, you will be able to cross off one of the items from your task list, something everyone enjoys.

78: Plan your telephone calls so you reach people in their office

Studies have shown that the majority of people are in their offices between the hours of 8:30 a.m. and 11:30 a.m. Therefore, try to plan time for phone calls during the morning hours when you are most likely to reach the recipient. Otherwise you will have to leave a message and when they call back there is a good chance they will pull your focus away from another important task. Or you end up playing phone tag for days on end!

79: Check your messages daily when away from the office

When you are out of the office, or on vacation, check your voicemail and/or email at least once per day. This will save you a large amount of time when you return to the office or home from your vacation.

80: Keep telephone numbers handy

Keep a small telephone book of your important numbers with you at all times. Or include them in your cell phone if you prefer. This way, when you need to make an important call you do not need to waste time trying to find the number, or calling people to get the numbers.

81: Always carry a small notebook in your purse, car or pocket

This way, when you think of something that needs to be done or something that you want or need to remember, you will be able to write it down and have it at your fingertips.

82: Eliminate extra seating in your office or workspace

This will help to minimize interruptions, and if you are interrupted you should stand to speak with whoever has come in. This will keep them standing, and minimize the time of the interruption.

83: Don't leave messages for people

If you make a phone call and the recipient is not there when you call, try asking when it might be better to try again instead of leaving a message for a return call. This is better than having someone return a call at a bad time for you, and it's certainly easy enough to put a small reminder in your planner to call back at a better time.

84: If possible, try to go into work earlier than others in the office or stay later

This will give you more quiet time during which you can get your work accomplished. And you are unlikely to be interrupted by co-workers or phone calls during extended hours.

85: Use a system to keep track of what needs to be done

Try keeping an index card for each day, placing the date in the top right corner before writing anything else on the card. On this card, record the top three things that you need to do during the day, and if there is room record what else you did during the course of the day. Then, file the card in an index card box at the end of the day. This is an excellent way to remember what you need to do, and what you have done on any given day.

86: Take time to occasionally review your goals, and to reassess their priority

This will allow you to remember what it is that you are working toward, and see whether you are actually progressing toward your goals. You might also discover that your priorities have changed over time, and that you need to set some new goals. By doing this you can keep your focus on tasks that are most important.

87: Spend fifteen minutes on planning before bed

All it takes is fifteen minutes of planning in the evening before you go to bed to significantly reduce the amount of planning that you will need to do the next morning. Give yourself the time necessary to prioritize, and to determine what you will need to have on hand for the following day. You'll probably find that before bed you're calmer and more able to focus on planning then you are in the morning when you're worried about starting your day.

88: Don't create an elaborate, difficult to follow system

The more hoops you have to jump through to make your time management system work, the more it becomes too time consuming. Instead focus on a simple system that works for you. If that's a daily to-do-list written with pen and paper then that's what you should use. The key is to find what is most effective at keeping you on track and sticking with it until using the system becomes a habit.

89: Make a list of your most important goals

Sit down and decide what exactly are the most important things to you. Raising healthy kids? Working toward a promotion? Helping others? Then evaluate every task against that list of goals. If a task doesn't bring you closer to achieving one of your goals then eliminate it or put it away for a rainy day when you have extra time. Sure the bathroom may need to be painted, but it really isn't a priority if you're so strapped for time that you're eating fast food every night.

90: Don't waste time talking to telemarketers

Do you get daily phone calls from telemarketers? Put a stop to it! In the US you can ask to be put on the "Do Not Call List". This is a national list that reputable telemarketing companies subscribe to. If you are on the list, they won't contact you. And if they do, you can file a complaint against them. Register your home and mobile phone numbers for free at http://www.donotcall.gov. This may not eliminate all unwanted phone calls, but it will significantly reduce the number.

91: Combine activities

Whenever possible, complete two activities at once. If you commute to work, spend that time listening to recorded training sessions. While you're waiting for your kids to finish swimming lessons complete your to-do-list. Or pay your bills while you watch your favourite television program. By combining these tasks you can get more done in less time!

92: Do it now

You have no doubt heard the old saying "why do today what you can put off until tomorrow". If this sounds like you then make it a goal to do things NOW instead of putting them off. If you are talking to someone and they say "Give me a call later in the week and we will set that up" respond by telling them

"Let's do it now instead and save ourselves making another call." Doing this will save you from wasting unnecessary time later playing phone tag. Otherwise a task that should take a minute or two ends up taking ten or fifteen minutes.

93: Be on the lookout for tasks you're doing over and over again

For example, are you always stopping to look up a certain number in the phonebook? Write it on the inside of the front cover instead. Are you constantly searching for your keys? Hang a hook by the front door. By eliminating these major time wasters you're creating more time in your schedule to get important tasks done.

94: Slow it down

Don't feel that you always have to be rushing around to be getting things done. Being productive doesn't mean going fast. What's key is that you're using your time wisely to complete the most important tasks. If you have to run around like a lunatic to get things done then you need to prioritize and focus on only a few items each day. By doing the most important things first you'll feel less of a time crunch.

95: Complete your least favourite task first

On almost every to-do-list there is something that you don't want to do. Instead of pushing it to the end of the list and wasting time and energy worrying about it – just do it! You will feel great once you have gotten it out of the way and everything else will seem easy by comparison.

96: Don't be too accessible

Cells phones, PDAs, email accounts… it seems that there is no end to the technology that is supposed to make our lives easier. In reality, it tends to make most people's lives more hectic then they need to be. Does this sound familiar… you have got your errands planned out and half way through you gets a call on your mobile phone from someone asking you to stop and pick up something else. Your entire schedule now has to be rearranged. It is convenient for the person who got out of doing that task for him or herself but not so great for you! When you have important tasks to complete leave the mobile phone and PDAs behind.

97: Leave time in your schedule for unexpected events.

It is never a good idea to fill your day completely. You never know what emergency or opportunity will come up that requires your focus. Leave a little room for these occurrences and they won't become a major source of stress.

98: Look for ways to spend more time on your most important tasks

Most people only spend one quarter of their time on the tasks they consider to be the most important to them. Take the time to monitor how much of your time goes to your most important tasks. Then look for ways to improve that to one third or even half of your time. You will be significantly more productive.

99: Get some things done before you open your email

For most people, email is a big time waster. And it often adds several items to your to-do-list. So instead of checking your email first thing in the morning, start your day by getting a couple of important tasks completed.

100: Use the most efficient method of communication

Unless you type several hundred words per minute, email is not an efficient method of communication. If you need to discuss something with someone give them a call or talk to them face to face. You can usually accomplish in a few minutes what it may take days of back and forth emails to get done.

101: Focus on one task at a time

Sure you may be a great multi-tasker, but the reality is that you will never be as productive as you can be if you are trying to do more than one thing at once. So focus on the task at hand and complete it before starting something else.

Chapter 17: Reducing Stress Through Time Management

Being disorganized is one of the common causes of stress. Time management is the key to organize your work at home and at the workplace, thus lessening the stress you may feel. Prioritizing the most important job and writing down you duties and activities everyday is the proper way of managing you time.

Keeping a diary or journal, where you can list down your objectives, can help you assess which duty must be done first and the estimated time you can accomplish each activity. Having a schedule can also help you provide the reason when your boss gives you unreasonable tasks.

Scheduling and Listing

If you feel you are going to have another busy day either at home or at work, always write down you tasks. Will you do the grocery first? What time will you pick up your kid at home? Sometimes, giving time even to tiniest task for the day can provide you time allowance to perform your other task. You must learn to prioritize to successfully beat stress.

Everyday pick the most important task you need to complete and finish it. If you are new in making lists, never put more than five things in your list. That way, you are more likely to finish all your tasks for the day, and provide you the feeling of accomplishment and greater sense of control. Then, by the time you are getting the hang of things, move on to making your second five-item list.

Learn to delegate to lessen your work. Sometimes, there are days where you think you have too many things to do but have so little time. During these days, make a list of the things that you can delegate to family members or co-workers. By delegating, you can surely avoid stress from building up.

In the workplace, learn to say no when you find yourself in the situation where you cannot handle anymore task than you already have. There are others who cannot fully assert their own capabilities and ends up being more stressed out than others who know their limitations.

These people also often end up having even more things to do. If you are having the trouble saying no, starting small is always the best choice. In events when you have so many things to do and your boss asks you to perform even more tasks, give your boss the choice of what thing he will allow you to do first.

Tell him that you cannot perform the task he asks you to do without giving up your task at hand. Even bosses can take the hint. At home, ask your husband or wife to make their own sandwich if you cannot find the time to do that for them or ask your daughter if her friends can give her a ride home after soccer practice. All these simple requests to others who ask so much of you can help you in lessening the stress that you can encounter.

Other Time Management Tips

People who are perfectionists often cannot help it if they feel stress at the end of each day. If you are a perfectionist, prioritize the task that needs meticulous attention to detail and finish it first. Always accomplish the items in your first list first before moving on to the second. This way you can avoid jumping from one list to another.

Everyday, remember that you need time to rest and relax for a while. Include in the list your work breaks and as much as possible, to things that would physically and mentally take you away from you work. Lastly, try not to make major decisions when you feel overworked or anxious.

Chapter 18: "Who's the Boss?" 10 Ways to Start Taking Control (Time Management, Goal Setting, Record Tracking)

At first glance, it would seem that positive thinking and Attention Deficit Disorder (ADD) have nothing to do with one another. But many of us with ADD develop negative thinking patterns because we become frustrated by our challenges and frequent feelings of being overwhelmed. This negative outlook then makes it even harder for us to manage those challenges and move forward.

Practicing positive thinking allows people with ADD to focus on our strengths and accomplishments, which increases happiness and motivation. This, in turn, allows us to spend more time making progress, and less time feeling down and stuck. The following tips provide practical suggestions that you can use to help you shift into more positive thinking patterns:

1. Take Good Care of Yourself It's much easier to be positive when you are eating well, exercising, and getting enough rest.

2. Remind Yourself of the Things You Are Grateful For Stresses and challenges don't seem quite as bad when you are constantly reminding yourself of the things that are right in life. Taking just 60 seconds a day to stop and appreciate the good things will make a huge difference.

3. Look for the Proof Instead of Making Assumptions A fear of not being liked or accepted sometimes leads us to assume that we know what others are thinking, but our fears are usually not reality. If you have a fear that a friend or family member's bad mood is due to something you did, or that your co-workers are secretly gossiping about you when you turn your back, speak up and ask them. Don't waste time worrying that you did something wrong unless you have proof that there is something to worry about.

4. Refrain from Using Absolutes Have you ever told a partner "You're ALWAYS late!" or complained to a friend "You NEVER call me!"? Thinking and speaking in absolutes like 'always' and 'never' makes the situation seem worse than it is, and programs your brain into believing that certain people are incapable of delivering.

5. Detach From Negative Thoughts Your thoughts can't hold any power over you if you don't judge them. If you notice yourself having a negative thought, detach from it, witness it, and don't follow it.

6. Squash the "ANTs" In his book "Change Your Brain, Change Your Life," Dr. Daniel Amen talks about "ANTs" - Automatic Negative Thoughts. These are the bad thoughts that are usually reactionary, like "Those people are laughing, they must be talking about me," or "The boss wants to see me? It must be bad!" When you notice these thoughts, realize that they are nothing more than ANTs and squash them!

7. Practice Lovin', Touchin' & Squeezin' (Your Friends and Family) You don't have to be an expert to know the benefits of a good hug. Positive physical contact with friends, loved ones, and even pets, is an instant pick-me-up. One research study on this subject had a waitress touch some of her customers on the arm as she handed them their bills. She received higher tips from these customers than from the ones she didn't touch!

8. Increase Your Social Activity By increasing social activity, you decrease loneliness. Surround yourself with healthy, happy people, and their positive energy will affect you in a positive way!

9. Volunteer for an Organization, or Help another Person Everyone feels good after helping. You can volunteer your time, your money, or your resources. The more positive energy you put out into the world, the more you will receive in return.

10. Use Pattern Interrupts to Combat Rumination If you find yourself ruminating, a great way to stop it is to interrupt the pattern and force yourself to do something completely different. Rumination is like hyper-focus on something negative. It's never productive, because it's not rational or solution-oriented, it's just excessive worry. Try changing your physical environment - go for a walk or sit outside. You could also call a friend, pick up a book, or turn on some music.

When it comes to the corporate world, protocol is pretty much the religion. To know the things needed to do are the basics of productivity, but interaction and having a steady mind makes up the entire thing to true productivity. There are those who seem to work well even under pressure, but they are uncommon ones and we are human and imperfect. To get these little things like stress under our skins won't solve our problems. Sometimes it takes a bit of courage to admit that we are turning to be workaholics than tell ourselves that we are not doing our best.

Chapter 19: What Can Time Management Bring to Your Personal Growth

The Key to a Better Life

Time management is basically about being focused. The Pareto Principle also known as the '80:20 Rule' states that 80% of efforts that are not time managed or unfocused generates only 20% of the desired output. However, 80% of the desired output can be generated using only 20% of a well time managed effort. Although the ratio '80:20' is only arbitrary, it is used to put emphasis on how much is lost or how much can be gained with time management.

Some people view time management as a list of rules that involves scheduling of appointments, goal settings, thorough planning, creating things to do lists and prioritizing. These are the core basics of time management that should be understood to develop an efficient personal time management skill. These basic skills can be fine tuned further to include the finer points of each skill that can give you that extra reserve to make the results you desire.

But there are more skills involved in time management than the core basics. Skills such as decision making, inherent abilities such as emotional intelligence and critical thinking are also essential to your personal growth.

Personal time management involves everything you do. No matter how big and no matter how small, everything counts. Each new knowledge you acquire, each new advice you consider, each new skill you develop should be taken into consideration.

Having a balanced life-style should be the key result in having personal time management. This is the main aspect that many practitioners of personal time management fail to grasp.

Time management is about getting results, not about being busy.

The six areas that personal time management seeks to improve in anyone's life are physical, intellectual, social, career, emotional and spiritual.

1. The physical aspect involves having a healthy body, less stress and fatigue.
2. The intellectual aspect involves learning and other mental growth activities.
3. The social aspect involves developing personal or intimate relations and being an active contributor to society.
4. The career aspect involves school and work.
5. The emotional aspect involves appropriate feelings and desires and manifesting them.
6. The spiritual aspect involves a personal quest for meaning.

Thoroughly planning and having a set of things to do list for each of the key areas may not be very practical, but determining which area in your life is not being giving enough attention is part of time management.

Each area creates the whole you, if you are ignoring one area then you are ignoring an important part of yourself.

Personal time management should not be so daunting a task. It is a very sensible and reasonable approach in solving problems big or small.

A great way of learning time management and improving your personal life is to follow several basic activities.

One of them is to review your goals whether it be immediate or long-term goals often.
A way to do this is to keep a list that is always accessible to you.

Always determine which task is necessary or not necessary in achieving your goals and which activities are helping you maintain a balanced life style.

Each and everyone of us has a peek time and a time when we slow down, these are our natural cycles. We should be able to tell when to do the difficult tasks when we are the sharpest.

Learning to say "No". You actually see this advice often. Heed it even if it involves saying the word to family or friends.

Pat yourself at the back or just reward yourself in any manner for an effective time management result.

Try and get the cooperation from people around you who are actually benefiting from your efforts of time management.

Don't procrastinate. Attend to necessary things immediately.

Have a positive attitude and set yourself up for success. But be realistic in your approach in achieving your goals.

Have a record or journal of all your activities. This will help you get things in their proper perspective.

These are the few steps you initially take in becoming a well rounded individual.

As they say personal time management is the art and science of building a better life.

From the moment you integrate into your life time management skills, you have opened several options that can provide a broad spectrum of solutions to your personal growth. It also creates more doors for opportunities to knock on.

Chapter 20: Benefits of Time Management

Our society is getting faster paced with each passing year. We are all looking for ways to help us complete the things that we need to do in the shortest time possible so that we can have additional time to have for ourselves. This can get us into trouble if doing things fast means that mistakes are made. When this happens we spend additional time correcting mistakes. This can create a vicious cycle. There are times when we simply need to slow things down.

One of the best things that we can do to help ourselves is to become more organized. Organization can help us manage our time better. There are many benefits of time management. We can be more productive as well as more efficient. When we are more efficient we save time and money. Other benefits of time management involve helping the company you work for save money. This creates a happy employer and when this reflects back to you, it may mean additional compensation in money or time off.

I think all of us realize the benefits of time management, but implementing the skills may be something new to us. I have found that lists work well for me. When I make lists at the end of each day I find I am more apt to get the things done that are needed the next day. My routine each night is to write down the things that I would like to as well as need to accomplish the next day. I then prioritize the list in order of what is most important to accomplish. Once this is done I look at any related tasks that can be done in conjunction with each other. For example if I need to meet with a co-worker on a different floor and also deliver reports to another department I will do this at the same time. This way I am away from my desk for one period of time thus cutting down on the amount of running around I need to do. I also do as much correspondence at one time as possible to limit the number of trips to the printer, copier and mail room. Multiple trips uses up time. Also I find when I am out and about away from my office I spend time greeting co-worker and doing other things that can eat away at my time.

Once my list is written and prioritized I begin with the top item and start working my way down. If I am on a tight schedule I limit the number of interruptions by putting my calls through to voice mail to answer later and also shut my office door. Whatever is not completed on my list by the end of the day gets added to the list for the next day. Some of these techniques may seem rigid, however the benefits of this time management pay off by getting things done and creating more time by the end of the week. Since I have been doing my work following these methods I find that I am often able to leave early at the end of the week.

Chapter 21: Time Management Strategies

Every one of us only has 24 hours in a day to work with. Hence, time management strategies allow you to accomplish more within a few hours, instead of having to extend your work on a single task for days. Here are a few strategies that you can apply to achieve that:

1: List down your activities

It need not be overemphasized that you have to learn how to prioritize your work. Meaning, you must set aside the less important tasks so you can focus on the more urgent ones. When you learn how to do this effectively, you can easily accomplish whatever it is you need to do within a shorter time. Make it a habit to write down a list of things to do. If you want to be really specific, break down all that you have to do within a day and in the order that you want them to get done.

As you list down your set of tasks to do, you have to identify which ones are long or short-term projects. Hence, you will be able to determine how much time you can allot for them within a day. A short-term task might be accomplished within, say a couple of hours. Meanwhile, for long-term tasks, you can try allotting 1 or 2 hours each day until when you intend to finish them. Hence, breaking down tasks would make it more efficient for you as you won't find it too strenuous.

2: Allocating time

Once you have your list, you now have to decide on how much time to allocate for each task or project you have set out to do for the day. Some tasks eat up a lot of time, so you have to be aware which are those. So as not to end up wasting so much time on one task, you have to provide time limits on each task so you can easily move on to the next.

When you do tasks in smaller chunks, it becomes a lot easier for you. Hence, you have eased yourself of the pressure. Instead, you can just focus on what you need to finish.

3: Know what you want to accomplish

Your 'to-do" list will serve as source of information for what your daily goals are. Hence, you can consult it to know what you have to do once you're through with one task.

There are a few questions that you can ask yourself: How much time are you willing to render for doing leisure activities? Are you willing to cut on the leisure time and appropriate more of them into your work so it can be more productive? Once you know what your goals are, you can use that as a motivation in order to finish the list that you have made.

4: Don't make your list of actions too long

When making your list, productivity is always on top of your mind. However, you should not try to make your list too long. Most people have this tendency but that is a common misconception. Doing more work at one time is not always equal to being productive.

Start off with a short list of the most important things you have to accomplish. That way, you can easily prioritize them. When you have already completed those on top of the list, you can always add a new set of activities.

When you try to put too many activities on your list, it may become too overwhelming for you. You could easily end up having to do several unfinished tasks at once. But that is not advisable. If you can or if it is within the time limits you have indicated for a certain task, try to complete it first before moving on to work on another one.

Chapter 22: Other Time Management Tools

While technology is at its most advanced state today, there remains to be a lot of things to juggle for a typical career-oriented individual. For most family-oriented people, there is the burden of juggling work, career, family and other factors involved in one's social life.

The answer is Time Management. Most successful people are often asked about what their secret to success is. And more often than not, they have the same response, and that is "time management". However, although this is almost an expected response, many are still baffled at how time management really works.

Time management is simply the proper allocation of time for certain priorities. First, the priorities have to be arranged in a certain way where it is clustered into sectors and listed according to urgency and importance. For example, the important parts of your life are career, your son, your home, your art, and your family. You have to know which one to drop first whenever you need to do something.

After that, you will need help from some time management tools designed to aid you in the correct process of prioritization AND remembering that order.

Quick-and-Easy Reminders

There are a lot of people who need lots of reminder when it comes to taking care of small businesses. Often, they are too small that they are disregarded as unimportant. If you are one of them, buy some quick-and-easy reminders. What's good about technology is you can probably put a reminder just about everywhere! Mobile phones nowadays have built-in organizers, post-its are available in different variants, and even the good old refrigerator door magnets have come in a lot of forms.

What is important is that the frequency of the reminding is now being increased. This is good for time management because it keeps you aware of the things which you have to do especially if they're urgent.

The Organizer + Watch Tandem

These are staples for just about every busybody – from the university beadle to the corporate leader. The organizer is something that holds your appointments and it's also a tiny little space for some writing. Busybodies usually have contact numbers of random people they meet, gifts for a not-so-relevant birthday party that he has to go to or some sudden brilliant ideas that come to mind. For these and more, you will need an organizer. It has to be a little notebook, just enough to fit in a handbag, and should be made of durable material. You must bring your organizer with you every day, in case you need to list something down as a reminder.

Moreover, the perfect complement to an organizer is a high-quality watch. You may have experienced running late for an appointment just because your watch didn't work well. What's worse is that the person you're meeting wouldn't even believe you. This blunder can easily be avoided. Just get a high quality watch. Having a good sense of time is practically the first step in time management.

The Perfect Mindset

It is pressuring to know that you have a lot of things in your hand and it seems like you can't even do anything about it. Don't tip over.

Moreover, keep a "be on your toes" kind of mindset as you maneuver your way into your busy life. Sure, there are times when you distance yourself from your organizer. For some, it is a painful reminder of the busy life they lead. It's perfectly alright to feel some form of eternal urgency but take some time off once in a while. You must never neglect yourself in your list of priorities.

Chapter 23: How to Teaching Time Management to Students

When you were a child, you never give importance to time. You were idle most of the time, reclining in bed, watch TV programs for so many hours, and sometimes amuse yourself with video games. As you become older, you will be remembering the things that you have accomplished. And you realized that you have not really achieved anything worthwhile.

One of our most priceless resources is Time. It is something that you can no longer reclaim, once you lost it. You should make use of your time intelligently. The reason is for your growth and improvement as a person. You always take a look for the wonderful memories and actions, which you have fulfilled. Remember that a well spent time is more precious than gold; hence, the need for time management.

Do you consider time management a basic concern for your students? What are some of the obstacles which stop them from finishing their assignments from school? Time management is indeed a problem for students.

Usually, it is due to their hectic schedules and social obligations from their peers. There are still very few people who could master this skill of time management. However, it a general need for everyone especially if you are aspiring to achieve something in school, work and other personal endeavours.

Students are supposed to manage their schedule properly. They are expected to attend their classes, perform their homework at home. Students should not postpone and entertain some distractions and interruptions. Otherwise, they will not be able to accomplish their academic obligations. Most of the time, these are difficult to fulfill.

However, do not feel bad about it. It is not the end of everything. You are not alone in this situation. Don't you know that majority of adults have the same problems on how to manage their time? There is still room for improvement. What is necessary now is to re-evaluate how you have been coming up with your daily activities and to modify them.

The students cannot do it alone. There is a need for somebody to teach and guide them. Based from the regular class schedule, there are some activities for time management, which are integrated to the subject itself. One example is the "beat the clock lessons." We have the lesson called "time monsters" The students will work in teams for two minutes so as to see in their lives the time monsters (time wasters) in a sheet of paper. Aside from that, they will learn the acronym "CHOICE".

1. Compare all your activities you would like to achieve
2. How you will be affected by your choice later on.
3. Order all your priorities in life.

4. Inscribe in your planner your desired schedule.
5. Carry out whatever desired plan you have formulated.
6. Enjoy every moment of your life as you manage your time.

There are some questions for discussion, like for example, the meaning of the word "procrastination" Some tips for time management are also provided according to whatever category you belong.

We have several essential principles of Time Management which students can use

1. List down all the things you are supposed to do everyday.
2. You should know when is the most conducive time for you to study.
3. The difficult subjects must be studied first.
4. Make use of your spare time.
5. There should be proper distribution of learning and practice.
6. The surroundings must be favourable for studying.
7. Do not be afraid to say no to somebody if it affects your schedule.
8. You should combine some activities so as to save time.
9. Allot some time for relaxation and entertainment.
10. You should have the required number of hours for sleeping and eat your food properly.
11. You should know your body clock so as to identify the best time for you to work.

12. Make it a habit to review your notes daily.
13. You should inform your friends about your schedule in order to avoid distractions.
14. Always be a taskmaster as you schedule your activities properly.
15. Do not waste your time by worrying about something that you are expected to be doing, just do it.
16. You should always keep things in their proper perspective.
17. You can entrust a responsibility when it is proper.
18. Relax and be calm always
19. Avoid being a perfectionist.
20. You are supposed to question everything that is included in your schedule.
21. Be a fast reader and be selective with what you read.
22. Make use of a calendar.

Chapter 24: Conclusion

Throughout the course of history mankind has sought to develop new ways to record, track and make better use of time. From the invention of the sundial to the introduction of the modern calendar, the need to responsibly understand and manage time has been a concern to individuals, both in their professional and personal lives, for thousands of years.

Modern methods of time management incorporate various ways of recording time, to help an individual identify barriers to the effective use of time. Long and short term goal setting is encouraged. The term time management also applies to any number of methods which may be employed to help an individual organize and prioritize the goals to be accomplished.

Popular methods of time management practiced in the 21st century include the Pareto Analysis, and Time Boxing, among a myriad of others. Each method proposes its own unique system to help the individual user manage time in a more orderly and productive fashion.

Tools used in time management may include either traditional or digital resources, such as planners, organizers, and or calendars. Additionally, goal setting outlines and specific formulas, which include various methods for prioritizing and organizing goals, are also used to assist in the effective management of time.

Time management techniques may also assist individuals in pinpointing and eliminating habits that interfere with the productive use of time.

At the same time, many methods provide insight into the development of new and better habits, which increase the rate of performance, and the ability of the individual to achieve goals on a regular basis.

Good Luck!

www.ingramcontent.com/pod-product-compliance
Lightning Source LLC
Chambersburg PA
CBHW051718170526
45167CB00002B/713